Duden, Jane
ATOS BL 5.2
Points: 1.0

MG

# Earthquake!

## On Shaky Ground

by Jane Duden

**Perfection Learning®**

Cover Photograph:  U.S. Geophysical Data Center
Inside Illustration:  Randy Messer, Mike Aspengren, Larry Nolte
Photo Sources:  American Red Cross, Library of Congress, U.S. Army
Corps of Engineers, U.S. Geophysical Data Center

## About the Author

As a freelance writer and former elementary teacher in Minnesota and Germany, Jane Duden has written 28 nonfiction books for children. She writes for teachers and kids on many topics but with great enthusiasm for animals, science, and the environment. Her quest for stories and adventures has taken her to every continent, including Antarctica. At home, she likes cooking, swimming, biking, in-line skating, and learning new things. She enjoys speaking at schools because she likes the spirit and sharing of young authors.

Jane lives in Minneapolis with a houseful of pets. She took a special interest in writing *Earthquake!* because her daughter attends Stanford University, which is located in a California earthquake zone.

# Table of Contents

# Introduction

It is January 17, 1994. The time is 4:31 a.m. Like many in the Los Angeles area, Greg Guler is asleep. But not for long. "Suddenly, it felt like a freight train was coming through the bedroom. Mostly I remember how loud it was—the roar of it. I just lay in bed and watched everything shake.

"It seemed like it went on for a long time. But it was only about ten seconds. I had a bookcase tip over. But just two blocks down from where I live, everything got trashed. I looked for fire and smelled for gas—in case the stove had broken away from the wall."

Greg says more. "Until you're *in* one, you don't ever think there's going to *be* one. I looked outside, and the water in the pool was sloshing around. It was like a giant playing with a pan of water. We didn't know right away how bad it was."

Greg is new to California. He recently moved from Minnesota to be an artist at Walt Disney Studios. When Greg went back to work after the quake, his paints were all over the floor. Thousands of other people were not so lucky.

This quake—Greg Guler's first—made headlines all over the world. The worst damage was in the Los Angeles suburb of Northridge, about 40 miles from the city.

So you think the earth under you is solid? People who have been in an **earthquake** know otherwise! An earthquake can cause a gentle rolling and shaking. Or a sudden, hard jolt. It can feel like walking on jelly. Or standing on a roller coaster. And it can cause death and destruction.

# Chapter 1

# What Makes the Earth Quake?

## Our Restless Earth

People don't expect the ground to jolt, shake, sway, and roll. But that's exactly what happens in an earthquake.

Just why do earthquakes happen? Earthquakes are caused by forces deep in the earth. These forces are always at work on rocks near the surface—squeezing and stretching them. When forces build up, the earth's rock-hard **crust** snaps and breaks. We feel the jolt as an earthquake.

Although many people will never experience one, earthquakes are very common on this planet. In fact, thousands occur each day, about once every 30 seconds.

Some earthquakes may be too small to be felt. Others may shake houses, rattle windows, and toss small objects. Or one may cause death and destruction. The problem is predicting where and when the big ones will occur.

## Earthquake Myths and Legends

Long ago, no one knew what caused the earth to shake. People told stories to explain it. Some people thought the earth rested on a turtle's back. So when the turtle moved, the earth shook.

Some believed a giant animal or god held the earth in place among the sun, moon, and stars. If the animal or god moved or sneezed, an earthquake happened.

Ancient Greeks thought a giant man called Atlas held the earth. So earthquakes happened when Atlas shrugged his shoulders.

An ancient Japanese legend said that a giant catfish thrashed about underground and made the earth shake. It was up to a certain god to keep the catfish calm.

Some people thought gases trapped in caves below the earth's surface caused quakes. The gases heated up and expanded. They pushed against the cave walls and made them move. Then the earth rolled and quaked.

Earthquakes were a mystery for centuries. But that changed around 1912 when scientists learned about **plate tectonics.**

The earth's crust is made of big **plates** that are always moving. *Plate tectonics* is the science that deals with this movement of the earth's crust. This science helps explain earthquakes.

# The Earth's Layers

Most people think of the earth as solid. But it's not. The inside of the earth is more like the cheese in a grilled-cheese sandwich.

Think of the earth as a huge ball with layers.

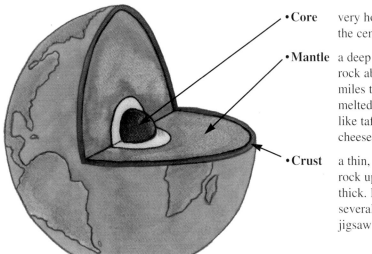

**•Core**    very hot rocks deep in the center of the earth

**•Mantle**    a deep layer of melted rock about 1,800 miles thick. This melted rock is soft like taffy or melted cheese.

**•Crust**    a thin, hard layer of rock up to 44 miles thick. It is made up of several pieces, like a jigsaw puzzle.

## Crustal Plates

Scientists believe that the earth's crust is many large slabs of rock. Each piece is called a *plate*. The plates float like giant rafts on the **mantle.**

Some plates slowly grind alongside others. Some crash together. In some places, the hot mantle oozes up between the plates. It pushes the plates apart and squeezes them together.

All this squeezing, stretching, bumping, and scraping builds up stress and strain. When the pressure is too much, the plates snap free with a jerk. This is the jolt we feel as an earthquake. The pressure may not all be released with the first quake. Then smaller earthquakes called *aftershocks* follow.

# Earth's Major Plates

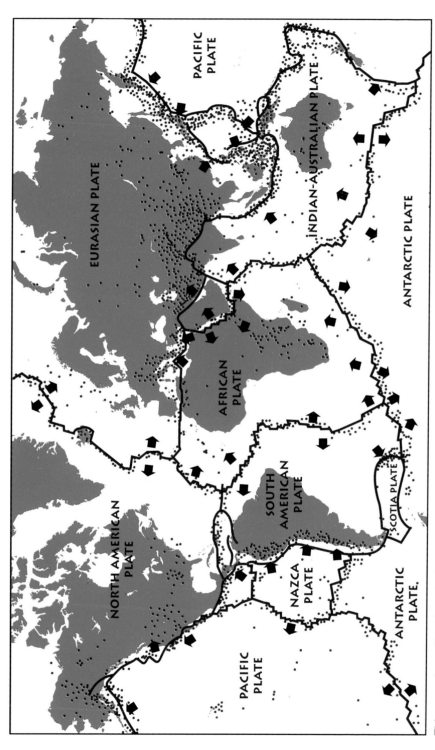

This map shows the plates in the earth's crust. Scientists named the plates. Much of the United States sits on the North American plate. Arrows show how experts think the plates are moving. The red data show where earthquakes happen.

# Try This!

1. Cook a hard-boiled egg. Imagine that it's the earth.

2. Tap the egg once or twice on a table. The shell will break into a few large sections. Your egg is now a model of the earth with its thin, rocky crust broken into plates.

3. What happens when you put force on the earth's crust? Hold the egg between both hands and gently push the egg at the ends. What happens to the "plates"?

4. Place the egg on a table and gently push the egg in the center. What happens to the plates? Do the plates lift up and shove under, bumping and grinding along the edges? Did you see new cracks as you forced the plates around?

The earth's crust suffers the same kinds of stresses, strains, slips, and jolts.

## Plate Boundaries

Crustal plates lie under the land. Strain builds up where the plates meet. Earthquakes happen most along plate boundaries.

Crustal plates also form the ocean floor. So sometimes earthquakes happen there.

Earthquakes also occur, but not as often, within plates. Stresses deep in the crust or along the plate edges can break these weak parts.

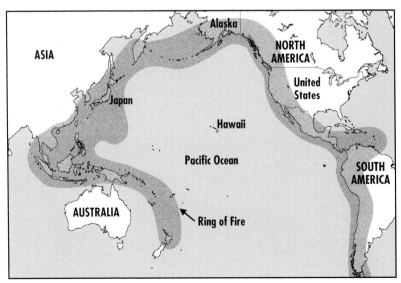

The edges of several plates almost encircle the Pacific Ocean. This area is called the **"Ring of Fire."** Many volcanoes and earthquakes happen there. In fact, 3/4 of the world's quakes occur there!

# Chapter 2

# What Are Faults?

## Faults: On Shaky Ground

A *fault* is a crack in the earth's crust. Faults can occur at plate boundaries or within plates. Faults are divided into three main groups by how they move.

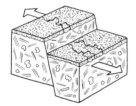

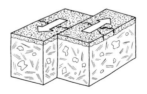

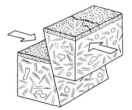

*Normal fault*  *Strike-slip fault*  *Thrust fault*

- *Normal* faults occur when rocks suddenly pull apart.

- *Strike-slip* (lateral) faults occur when two slabs of rock try to scrape past each other.

- *Thrust* (reverse) faults occur when chunks of rock press together and force one side over the other. Thrust faults break the earth's surface.

# Try This!

How can forces build up enough to break solid rock and jerk it into a new position?
1. Press your hands together with your palms touching.
2. Push one palm hard against the other. At the same time, press the other palm hard in the opposite direction.
3. Press hard until your palms slip with a sudden jerk.
Imagine the force of the earth's plates as they grind into each other in this way!

## Hidden Faults

Many faults are well known. But not all. Some faults don't show. *Blind faults,* or *hidden faults,* lie deeply buried.

**Seismologists** have known about blind thrust faults for some time. But they didn't worry about them.

Then came the big Coalinga quake of 1983. It happened in a part of central California with no faults that broke the ground.

Ross Stein is a geophysicist with the U.S. Geological Survey (U.S.G.S.). He told *Discover* magazine, "We knew then that we had been missing one of the major sources of earthquakes."

People in Northridge, California, had no idea that a deadly fault lay right below them, 9 miles down. They found out the hard way when the earth moved at 4:31 a.m. on January 17, 1994.

## Some Famous Faults

Many faults are inactive. Others are very active. Scientists have found that earthquakes tend to reoccur along fault lines.

**San Andreas**

The San Andreas fault is California's main quake-maker. It winds more than 700 miles through southern California. It runs from north of San Francisco, past Los Angeles, and into northern Mexico. Just north of San Francisco, it dives under the Pacific Ocean.

The fault cuts under houses and towns. It runs through deserts and farms. It slashes through cities where millions of people live.

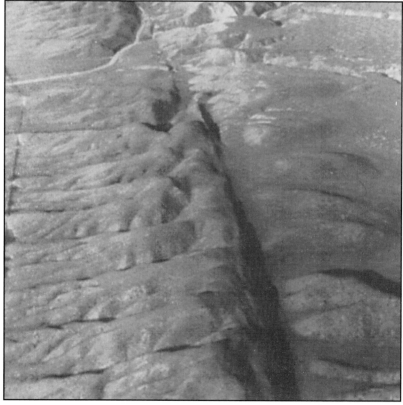

San Andreas fault in central California

Dozens of small quakes happen along the San Andreas fault each year. Many scientists think that a giant, deadly superquake will strike along this fault before the year 2000.

The San Andreas fault lies between two plates. These grind against each other in a strike-slip movement.

The land and sea west of the fault include Los Angeles and San Diego. This land rides on the Pacific plate and moves northwest.

Land east of the fault sits on the North American plate. This plate moves southeast.

The plates slide past each other in northern and southern California. Near Los Angeles they ram into each other.

**Elysian Park**

The Elysian Park web of faults spreads under Los Angeles. Twelve million people live in the area. Geologists say that dozens of faults may slice through rock under Greater Los Angeles.

Many are blind thrust faults. We can't see these faults. So geologists don't know that faults are there until a quake occurs. Geologists say a quake three times as powerful as the 1994 Northridge quake is likely to hit Los Angeles before the year 2025.

**New Madrid**

California isn't the only place where things are shaking. Another quake hot spot lies in the heart of the United States.

The New Madrid fault line is named for a tiny town in Missouri. The fault is 120 miles long. It starts in Cairo, Illinois. It travels south through Kentucky and Tennessee. The fault ends in Marked Tree, Arkansas.

Everyone in Marked Tree knows about the three big quakes of December 16, 1811. The quakes shook the land like a picnic blanket being flipped clean of crumbs.

Islands sank in the Mississippi River. The great river even leaped free of its banks, flowing north for a few hours.

Then in the next five months, some 2,000 quakes and shocks hit the area. Luckily, not many people lived in the region. Today, people along the New Madrid fault zone believe they are due for another big one. Seismologists agree.

New Madrid fault line

# Chapter 3

# Where Do Earthquakes Happen?

### Locating an Earthquake

An earthquake sends out shock waves in all directions from the point of the break. This point, where the earthquake starts, is called the *focus*. The focus can be anywhere between the earth's surface and 450 miles (280 km) below it.

The *epicenter* is the place on the earth's surface directly above the focus of an earthquake.

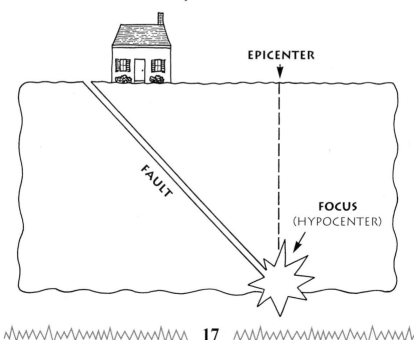

EPICENTER

FAULT

FOCUS
(HYPOCENTER)

# Earthquake Waves

Every quake has three kinds of shock waves or vibrations.

The first shock waves are **primary waves**—**P** waves. Their push-pull vibration travels directly through the earth.

Fast **P** waves push rocks and particles just ahead of themselves. This is the first jolt of a quake. Sometimes a **P** wave can be heard as a low rumble.

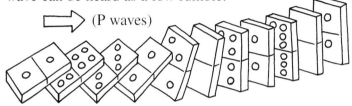

(P waves)

Next come the more powerful secondary waves—**S** waves. They are also called ***shear waves*** or *transverse waves.*

**S** waves move more slowly. They shove rocks and materials from side to side as they pass through the rock deep within the earth.

(S waves)

Other earthquake vibrations travel near the surface of the earth. These are ***Rayleigh*** **waves** (**R** waves) and ***Love*** **waves** (**L** waves.)

They are named after the scientists who discovered them. **R/L** waves move the slowest. They roll, sway, and shake the ground. **R/L** waves cause the most damage.

(R/L waves)

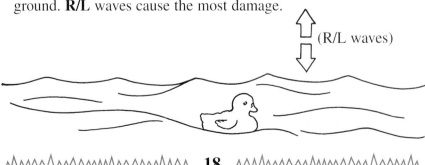

# Where Are You Safe from an Earthquake?

No place on Earth is totally safe from quakes. Earthquakes can happen in many places. But they are concentrated in certain areas. And some areas have almost no quakes.

Look at the list below. Which areas have the fewest earthquakes?

## EARTHQUAKES IN THE UNITED STATES, 1980–1994

| State | Number of Reported Quakes | Largest Magnitude (Richter Scale) |
|---|---|---|
| Alabama | 8 | 4.5 |
| Alaska | 14,254 | 7.9 |
| Arizona | 71 | 4.0 |
| Arkansas | 55 | 4.7 |
| California | 11,072 | 7.6 |
| Colorado | 109 | 4.6 |
| Connecticut | 6 | 3.8 |
| Delaware | 1 | 2.4 |
| Florida | 0 | — |
| Georgia | 9 | 3.2 |
| Hawaii | 200 | 6.7 |
| Idaho | 900 | 7.3 |
| Illinois | 26 | 5.1 |
| Indiana | 11 | 4.1 |
| Iowa | 0 | — |
| Kansas | 14 | 4.0 |
| Kentucky | 27 | 5.2 |
| Louisiana | 1 | 3.8 |
| Maine | 21 | 4.3 |
| Maryland | 9 | 2.7 |
| Massachusetts | 13 | 3.7 |
| Michigan | 2 | 3.6 |
| Minnesota | 2 | 4.1 |
| Mississippi | 2 | 2.9 |
| Missouri | 51 | 5.0 |
| Montana | 373 | 4.8 |
| Nebraska | 11 | 3.8 |
| Nevada | 650 | 6.3 |
| New Hampshire | 19 | 4.7 |
| New Jersey | 7 | 3.2 |
| New Mexico | 66 | 5.0 |
| New York | 27 | 5.3 |
| North Carolina | 14 | 3.5 |
| North Dakota | 1 | 3.3 |
| Ohio | 17 | 5.0 |
| Oklahoma | 108 | 3.7 |
| Oregon | 327 | 6.9* |
| Pennsylvania | 24 | 4.6 |
| Rhode Island | 2 | 2.7 |
| South Carolina | 29 | 3.5 |
| South Dakota | 14 | 4.6 |
| Tennessee | 52 | 4.3 |
| Texas | 32 | 3.9 |
| Utah | 273 | 5.9 |
| Vermont | 0 | — |
| Virginia | 6 | 3.5 |
| Washington | 668 | 5.5 |
| West Virginia | 2 | 3.5 |
| Wisconsin | 0 | — |
| Wyoming | 296 | 5.5 |

*This quake occurred in the Pacific Ocean about 70 miles off the coast of Oregon. The largest earthquake within Oregon during this time period was magnitude 4.3.

# Earthquake Zones in the United States

**DAMAGE**

- MAJOR
- MODERATE
- MINOR
- NONE

# The Quake That Didn't

Marked Tree, Arkansas, suffered in the big New Madrid quake. The local museum tells the story.

In 1990, the small town got ready for another big one. Dr. Iben Browning predicted a quake around December 3 of that year. Dr. Browning is a climate expert from New Mexico.

Some folks didn't believe him, but some did. Like the mayor of Marked Tree. He said, "I don't think it's gonna happen, but there's no need to take any chances."

Marked Tree got ready. The school had earthquake drills. The town made a list of people with two-way radios. They formed emergency rescue teams. People bought extra blankets, flashlights, and canned food.

Then they tried to relax. They even had a fault festival called "Quake, Rattle, and Roll."

But December came and went without a quake. The town museum still sells T-shirts with sayings like *It's Our Fault.*

# IT'S OUR FAULT

# New Discoveries

Today scientists have a better understanding of what causes earthquakes. But their ideas can change as they discover new information.

Some scientists now believe that human activities may trigger quakes. They say a 1993 earthquake in India may have been caused by the building of a dam. Mining and underground explosions could also trigger quakes.

Chapter

# What Happens When the Earth Moves?

## Earthquakes Damage and Destroy

An earthquake is a powerful force of nature. Sometimes an earthquake just shakes the ground. Other times it splits the rocks at the surface. Buildings shake—and they shatter. A quake can destroy in seconds what has taken years to build.

Powerful quakes can
- snap bridges
- buckle freeways
- twist train tracks like spaghetti
- cover streets with broken glass and rubble
- rupture gas mains and start fires
- cut off electricity and plunge cities into darkness
- crumble homes
- cause avalanches and slides, burying places under mud and rock

*Sand boils* sometimes bubble up during earthquakes. These are dangerous to buildings in places where there's underground water.

Homes destroyed during 1906 San Francisco earthquake

Sandy soil beneath the buildings turns to quicksand. The buildings lean or tip over. Parts of cities can sink when the soil drops away.

This happened in Japan in a 1964 earthquake. During the 1989 San Francisco quake, sand boils bubbled up like tiny volcanoes. They erupted in basements, in yards, and under houses.

## Earthquakes Cause Suffering

People and animals suffer because of earthquakes. Both can be injured or killed. Many people find themselves homeless. Many risk their lives to rescue others. And everyone is scared.

In the Northridge, California, quake of 1994, one child said, "I was scared. Nobody knew the quake was coming. Now everyone is getting prepared. Just in case it happens again."

Fear after a big quake is normal for people of all ages. Many have nightmares. Others are edgy and quick to anger. Students can't concentrate. Workers have trouble keeping their minds on their jobs.

The Northridge quake brought more than 5,000 aftershocks. So people have stayed scared. One woman sleeps on the kitchen floor, ready to roll under the table when necessary. Some people keep hard hats or heavy salad bowls next to their beds to use as helmets.

After a quake, many workplaces hire crisis counselors. They talk to people for weeks. They listen to people's fears. They help them cope.

## Earthquakes Cause Tsunamis

Now and then, underwater quakes cause giant ocean waves. Some people call them "killer waves." The correct name for these megawaves is *seismic sea waves*. The Japanese name for the waves is *tsunami*.

At sea, a tsunami looks like a harmless hump of fast-moving water, 2–3 feet (0.6–0.9 m) high. A tsunami can race at speeds up to 500 miles per hour (800 km/hr).

In shallow water close to shore, the racing water slows down and piles up. Then it bashes the coast with deadly force. Tsunamis can be 50–125 feet high. You can imagine the force in such a huge wall of water!

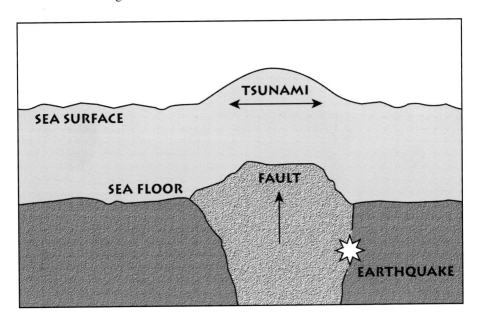

Hawaiian beach engulfed by tsunami wave

Tsunamis can strike without warning. They can be started by a quake hundreds or thousands of miles from where they strike. So there is no way to tell when one will arrive onshore.

In 1896, a sea wave over 70 feet high drowned about 26,000 people in Honshu, Japan. In 1964, a giant wave swept over Crescent City, California. This tsunami killed 119 people.

The 1964 earthquake in Alaska caused seismic sea waves. The focus of the quake was deep under the waters of Prince William Sound. Tsunamis battered the Alaskan coast for hours. The huge waves raced across the Pacific at hundreds of miles per hour. They reached Hawaii. They even reached Japan— 4,000 miles away.

Today, tsunami warning centers help save lives. Hawaii, Hong Kong, and other places have warning centers.

Workers at the centers watch for underwater seismic activity. This helps them predict where and when seismic sea waves might happen. Given time and warning, people can head for higher ground and safety.

# Chapter 5

# How Do Scientists Measure Earthquakes?

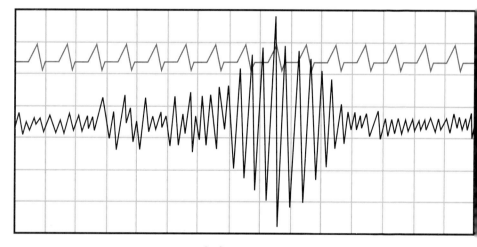

**Seismogram**

A *seismograph* shows how hard a quake shakes. It measures earthquake **tremors** or vibrations.

The energy of a quake is measured by how far the needle moves on a seismograph. The tremor shows as a wiggly line traced on a turning drum with chart paper attached. This leaves a written record of the quake called a **seismogram.** A modern seismograph can record a tiny earth tremor thousands of miles away.

Today, there are hundreds of seismograph stations all over the world. With more stations, more earthquakes are found. So far, that's about 19,000 quakes a year.

## Richter Scale

Scientists use special numbers to describe the size of earthquakes. The **Richter Scale** is the best-known scale for measuring earthquakes. The Richter Scale tells the amount of energy released when the earthquake takes place.

On the Richter Scale, 2.0 is feeble, just noticeable by some people. A 3.0 feels similar to the passing of heavy trucks. A 6.0 equals all the energy of 2,000,000 space shuttle liftoffs.

Any quake that registers 6.0 or more is considered a major quake. A 7.0 equals the energy given off by Niagara Falls in four months. An 8.0 equals the energy of the meteor that created a 570-foot-deep (190 m) crater in Arizona.

Each number on the Richter Scale stands for a quake that is 10 times more powerful than the number below it. An increase of one number on the Richter Scale means 10 times more ground motion and about 32 times more energy than the number below it.

For example, an 8.0 quake is over
- 30 times more powerful than a 7.0
- 900 times stronger than a 6.0
- 27,000 times mightier than a 5.0 quake!

## Moment-Magnitude Scale

Scientists now use a more precise scale called the **Moment-Magnitude Scale.** This scale measures total energy released by a quake. Experts multiply the area of the fault's rupture surface by the distance the earth moves along the fault.

moment magnitude = area of rupture x distance the earth moves

The table below shows how the Richter and the Moment-Magnitude scales compare.

| Earthquake | Richter Scale | Moment-Magnitude Scale |
|---|---|---|
| Chile, 1960 | 8.3 | 9.5 |
| Alaska, 1964 | 8.4 | 9.2 |
| New Madrid, 1811 | 8.7 | 8.1 |
| Michoacán, Mexico, 1985 | 8.1 | 8.1 |
| San Francisco, CA, 1906 | 8.3 | 7.7 |
| Loma Prieta, CA, 1989 | 7.1 | 7.0 |
| Kobe, Japan, 1995 | 7.8 | 6.9 |
| Northridge, CA, 1994 | 6.4 | 6.7 |

## Mercalli Intensity Scale

Richter Scale and Moment-Magnitude Scale measurements still don't tell the whole story. The effects of an earthquake depend on where the quake takes place. An earthquake in Antarctica does not damage the people or property that an earthquake in a crowded city does.

So the *Mercalli Intensity Scale* is useful to scientists. This scale measures the effects of an earthquake on people and property.

The Mercalli Scale rates quake damage from I to XII. A quake of I causes very little damage. At XII, damage is total. This rating depends upon eyewitness reports and field investigations.

For example, the earthquake that shook San Francisco in 1989 measured 7.1 on the Richter Scale. On the Mercalli Scale, it was X to XI in a part of the city where houses were built on loose soil. Damage was greater because of the softer ground. In other parts of the city where houses suffered less damage, the quake measured only VI or VII.

# Chapter 6

# What Makes an Earthquake Memorable?

## Classifying Earthquakes

Thousands of earthquakes occur every day. Most are so tiny that people can't feel them. Many happen under the ocean. Or in places far away from cities and people.

The worst quakes are the ones that strike crowded cities full of buildings that aren't built to take violent shaking. Those are the quakes we remember.

The following scale shows what the Richter Scale numbers mean.

**Magnitude Scale**
(Richter)
Less than 3 = very minor
3 to 3.9 = minor
4 to 4.9 = light
5 to 5.9 = moderate
6 to 6.9 = strong
7 to 7.9 = major
8 and above = great

Here are some famous earthquakes. The diagram on page 34 shows how they compare on the **magnitude** scale.

## San Francisco, California, 1906

San Francisco. 5:12 a.m. April 18, 1906. A section of rock on the San Andreas fault slipped.

The rumbling lasted 75 seconds. Gas mains broke, setting off fires. Fires raged for three days. Water mains also broke. So there was no water to fight the flames. More than 700 people died.

The violent quake was felt over an area twice the size of California. The city was left in ruins. 250,000 people were left homeless.

This quake happened before the Richter Scale was developed. Experts guess it was magnitude 8.3.

Fire and destruction following the 1906 San Francisco earthquake

## Tokyo, 1923

September 1 is the anniversary of the great 1923 Tokyo quake. More than 140,000 people died. On this day each year, Japanese schoolchildren practice earthquake drills.

After the 1923 quake that measured 8.3, Japan made some

big changes. The nation now stores a ten-day supply of water—about 400,000 tons—in earthquake-proof tanks in Tokyo. The water will help fight fires caused by quakes.

Stockpiles of food and blankets are waiting in case of disaster. Trained disaster teams are standing by.

Schools, offices, and factories hold regular earthquake drills. Posters, leaflets, and TV and radio ads teach people what to do if an earthquake strikes.

## Chile, 1960

All through a long and destructive week, Chile cracked and heaved. When the week finally ended, Chile had suffered a dozen earthquakes. The five biggest measured between 7.25 and 8.5 on the Richter Scale. Over a quarter of the country's population was left homeless.

The quakes struck along a fault line that cuts through Chile's wheat-growing breadbasket. The city of Concepción had been destroyed five times in the past by earthquakes. This time only the earthquake-proof buildings survived the first shudder.

In its wake, six old volcanoes and three new ones erupted. Huge seismic waves, tsunamis, caused damage across the Pacific.

## Alaska, 1964

The Alaskan quake of 1964 released twice as much energy as the 1906 San Francisco quake. It was so violent that the tops of trees snapped off. An elementary school was split in two when the ground beneath it dropped.

More than 100 people died. Some were as far away as California. Loss of life and property would have been much greater if more people lived in Alaska.

# Mexico City, Mexico, 1985

It was the morning of September 19, 1985. The day began as usual in Mexico City, the largest city in the western hemisphere.

Then a powerful 8.1 earthquake struck. It lasted two minutes. It left 4,000 people dead.

But that was only the beginning. The next day, a second mighty quake struck. It measured 7.3 on the Richter Scale.

Mexico City is built on the bed of an ancient lake. Because of the soft ground, many buildings were shaken off their foundations. Hundreds of homes, stores, hotels, hospitals, schools, and businesses were destroyed.

In all, 10,000 people died. Another 20,000 were hurt.

# Armenia, 1988

A deadly 6.9 earthquake hit Soviet Armenia in 1988. A 5.8 aftershock followed four minutes later. Dozens more quakes shook Armenia over the next months.

In all, there were 50,000 deaths. Many buildings fell because they were not built to stand up to an earthquake. As Dr. Roger Bilham of the University of Colorado told the *New York Times*, "It is buildings, not earthquakes, that kill people."

# California, 1989

The date was October 17, 1989. The third game of the World Series was about to start. San Francisco's Candlestick Park was packed.

Shortstop Walt Weiss stumbled while jogging in the outfield. "I thought I hit a hole in the ground," he told the Oakland *Tribune*. "I was going to start checking the grass, but everything else started moving too. Then I knew it was an earthquake."

The ground rolled in huge waves. People from Los Angeles to southern Oregon and western Nevada felt the quake. Part of the San Andreas fault had broken.

The Bay Bridge split. Interstate 880 in Oakland collapsed. Forty-four slabs of concrete deck, each weighing 600 tons, fell on cars below.

Within 15 seconds, the vibrations faded. But 63 persons lay dead or dying. Some 3,800 suffered injuries.

Thousands of homes and businesses were destroyed. A thousand other structures were damaged beyond repair. There were ten aftershocks of 3.5 or greater.

This quake is known as the Loma Prieta quake. It is named for the mountain near its epicenter.

The October 17, 1989, Loma Prieta earthquake caused the collapse of this highway overpass in Oakland, California.

## Magnitude Scale

| | |
|---|---|
| 9.5 | Chile, 1960 |
| 9.4 | |
| 9.3 | |
| 9.2 | Alaska, U.S., 1964 |
| 9.1 | |
| 9.0 | |
| 8.9 | Japan, 1933 |
| 8.8 | |
| 8.7 | |
| 8.6 | |
| 8.5 | |
| 8.4 | |
| 8.3 | Tokyo, 1923 |
| 8.2 | San Francisco, CA, 1906 |
| 8.1 | Mexico, 1985 |
| 8.0 | |
| 7.8 | Kobe, Japan, 1995 |
| 7.6 | Mexico, 1985 |
| 7.4 | |
| 7.2 | Loma Prieta, CA, 1989 |
| 7.0 | Armenia, 1988 |
| 6.5 | |
| 6.4 | Northridge, CA, 1994 |

## Northridge, California, 1994

A 6.7 quake struck Northridge, California, on January 17, 1994. Northridge is a suburb of Los Angeles. Cracks in the pavement opened and shu like huge jaws. It toppled ten highway bridges. It wrecked 3,000 homes. And i killed 60 people.

Corps inspectors examining Northridge apartments

## Kobe, Japan, 1995

Japan is prepared for quakes. It has one of the world's strictest building codes. But Japan is not quake-proof— nowhere is!

A 7.2 quake hit Kobe on January 1 1995. The quake shook Kobe with the force of 240 kilotons of TNT.

The quake lasted only 20 seconds. But 5,000 people were killed. 26,000 more were injured. It left 300,000 peop homeless.

# The Big Ten

The ten largest earthquakes in the 20th century are shown
on the world map below.

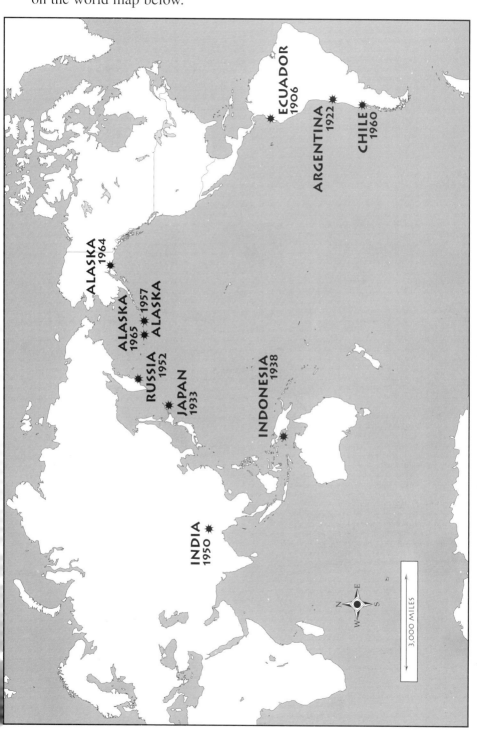

# Worst Quakes, 1556–1995

- **The Strongest:** Off the coast of Ecuador in 1906 and off the coast of Japan in 1933. Both quakes were 8.9 on the Richter Scale.

- **The Longest:** Anchorage, Alaska, 1964. The ground gently rolled for 40 seconds. Then it shook violently for four minutes. Aftershocks went on for nine months.

- **The Deadliest:** Shaanxi, China, 1556. Nearly 800,000 people died. Earthquake experts call this the greatest single disaster in history.

- **The Most Costly in U.S. History:** The 1994 Northridge, California, quake. It will cost Los Angeles at least $700 million just to repair 150 schools. Total damages were about $30 billion.

- **Most Violent in the United States:** Anchorage, Alaska, 1964. It registered 9.2 on the Richter Scale. In the first three days after the quake, 300 aftershocks rattled buildings still standing.

Costly damage caused by the January 17, 1994, Northridge earthquake

# Chapter 7

# Who's to the Rescue?

## Help from Computers

The hours after a major quake can mean no water, no electricity, no gas, no sleep. But rescue efforts must begin. Rescue workers need to know where to work. Colorful computer-generated maps help them.

Geographic Information Systems (GIS) turn numbers into charts and maps. The charts can offer details. The maps show which areas are hardest hit. In this way, help is sent to the neediest victims first.

Later, GIS maps can be used to analyze the damage. They show which building types and soil types did the best and the worst in the quake. This information helps improve building codes, which explain where and how to build.

## Help from FEMA

When disasters occur, the United States government sends help all over the country. The Federal Emergency Management Agency (FEMA) is the name of a government agency that sends help.

FEMA sends rescue workers and people to translate.

Soon FEMA building inspectors arrive on the scene. They go to homes and businesses to look at the damage. They send the facts by computer modem right to FEMA's computer center. They give out government money to help people start rebuilding.

Thanks to this speedy system, homeowners in the Northridge, California, quake got money for emergency repairs within six days rather than the usual 30 or 40.

## Help from Modern Equipment

Modern equipment aids in rescues. Searchers must first determine what's actually trapping the victim.

Rescue workers at the collapsed Northridge Meadows Apartments placed fiber-optic cables into holes in the rubble. The cables carried a light, a camera, and a microphone. In this way, workers found and talked to people trapped inside.

Then workers must decide whether to cut, bend, move, lift, or break things to free the trapped victim. They use cranes and jackhammers to move rubble. They use airbags that are like pillows to lift heavy walls, beams, and posts high enough to save a life.

## Heroes and Helpers

An earthquake is always followed by cries for help. Injured people need doctors and nurses. They need clothing, blankets, food, and medical supplies. They need trained people to take down damaged buildings safely. Or put up electric power lines.

Who comes to the rescue? Police, firefighters, and government employees work day and night. Neighbors risk their own safety to pull others from smashed homes. They listen for any sound of human life.

Using cranes, pickaxes, or bare hands, volunteers rescue victims caught under the rubble. They work where danger is still high. Volunteers also donate blood for injuries.

Search dogs help at many rescue sites. Kids help too. Following the Mexico City quake, Boy Scouts helped at first-aid stations and rescue sites. They collected everything from medicine to food and clothing.

Sometimes phone lines are down, electricity is out, and families are separated. People worry, "Is my family okay? Is it safe to stay in my house?"

Quake victims rely on cellular phones, beepers, and computer networks to reach each other. If one system doesn't work, another one might.

Ham radio operators come to the rescue too. They send reports. They contact people's friends and relatives. They can do this because they have generators to power their radios.

Chapter

# Can Earthquakes Be Predicted?

### Inventions Help Predict Quakes

When will the next big one happen? No one knows for sure. But scientists are working on it!

Earthquakes are so deadly because they strike without warning. With advance warning, lives could be saved. Property could be protected.

Scientists in the United States and Japan are inventing things that may help predict earthquakes. These are some ways that scientists try to keep ahead of quakes.

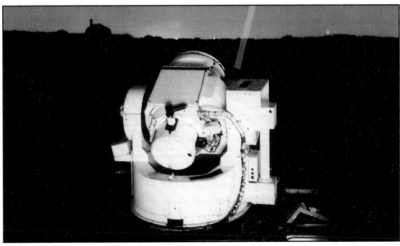

Satellites can measure even the smallest shifts in the earth's plates.

## • Lasers

Scientists send a beam of laser light across a fault line to a reflector. They time how long it takes for the laser beam to bounce off the reflector. This tells them about any movement of the ground along the fault.

## • Creepmeter

A creepmeter measures movement along a fault line. A weight on the end of a wire goes up or down as the fault moves.

## • Water Wells

Water wells provide clues. Scientists know that rock beneath a well is affected by forces in the earth. Instruments that record the level of groundwater are put in the wells. The instruments send the data to a satellite. Then it goes to experts for analysis. This helps scientists detect seismic activity.

## Scientists Study Quakes

The U.S. Geological Survey (U.S.G.S.) studies quakes. It is the nation's largest earth science research and information agency.

So far, seismologists can only predict that a quake is *likely*. They still can't tell exactly *where* or *when*.

Studying quakes helps people decide where it is safest to build homes, offices, and stores. It also helps people build structures that stand up better during quakes.

## • Scientists watch plates move.

The global positioning system (G.P.S.) is a network of satellites. The satellites measure movement of the earth's crust very closely. In this way, scientists know where quakes are likely. For example, G.P.S. numbers prove that land at the southern tip of Los Angeles is moving closer to Pasadena in the north by a third of an inch a year.

**• Scientists look for patterns in history.**
Seismologists study the times between earthquakes. Any patterns can help them make rough predictions.

**• Scientists also watch for warning signs from the earth.**
Certain things happen before an earthquake. Small tremors shake the ground gently. Swellings and cracks show up on the earth's surface. Water in ponds gives off strange smells. Radon emissions increase. Underground water level changes up and down. These signs alert seismologists to keep close watch.

**• Scientists use the seismic gap theory.**
They study how often the fault cracked in the past. That helps them figure out when it might crack again. This method predicted three earthquakes: Chile in 1985, Mexico in 1978, and Alaska in 1979.

If we could predict earthquakes, people would have avoided this Northridge freeway on the morning of January 17, 1994.

# Can Animals Predict Earthquakes?

Animals seem to know earthquakes are coming a long time before the earthquakes start. Zoo alligators normally sunbathe quietly. But Japanese zookeepers claim alligators will screech in a chorus before a major earthquake.

Dogs howl for no reason. Fish swarm shallow waters. Birds sing at night. Chickens refuse to roost. Mice and rats leave their hiding places.

In 1975, farm animals near Oroville, California, were acting strangely. Cattle stopped grazing and bellowed loudly. Horses ran wildly in their corrals. Dogs whined and howled. This went on for days. Then a major earthquake hit Oroville.

It was two weeks before the 1964 Alaska earthquake. Hibernating bears on Kodiak Island woke up and ran for the hills.

It's as though the animals say, "Get me out of here!" It appears that many critters are supersensitive to low rumblings and changes in the ground that come before quakes.

In December 1974, people near the Chinese town of Haicheng began to report odd animal behavior. Hundreds of thousands of people gave reports at this time. Many reports were about farm animals. More were about snakes. Thousands of snakes crawled out of their hibernation holes.

Chinese scientists feared a quake. So they ordered people to leave Haicheng. On February 4, 1975, a radio message sent the warning. An earthquake was coming!

At 7:30 that night, the city was destroyed by an earthquake. Because of the advance warning, fewer people died in this giant quake. This was the first time an earthquake of this size had been predicted correctly.

The Chinese have a folk verse about what animals do before earthquakes.

> Cattle, sheep, mules, and horses do not enter corrals.
> Rats leave their homes and flee.
> Hibernating snakes leave their burrows early.
> Frightened pigeons continuously fly and do not return to nests.
> Rabbits raise their ears, jump aimlessly, and bump things.
> Fish are frightened, jump above water surface.

## Chapter

# Can We Make Life Safer from Earthquakes?

### Where to Build

Until we learn to predict quakes, proper building design keeps people safer. In quake-prone areas, people know to build houses on solid rock. They use steel instead of brick or cement. They follow building codes.

Changes in building codes have helped many highways and buildings stand up to quakes. But each quake gives experts new information about what works and what doesn't.

### Steel Backbones

Steel is safer in a quake than unreinforced concrete or brick. So it has been the material of choice for many builders.

Flexible steel frames help buildings ride out earthquakes. If the ground shifts, the frame sways sideways.

But some building projects are on hold since the Northridge quake. **Civil engineers** are scrambling to figure out why steel welds cracked so often.

# Smart Buildings

The *smart building* is one of the newest ideas in quakeproofing. These buildings respond like living things to quake jolts.

A smart building has special sensors. These take note of ground vibrations. Then they send a message to a central computer—the building's "brain." Next, the computer tells the building to move in a way that offsets the forces of the earthquake.

Models of several smart systems are being tested. One system uses a huge weight on the top floor of a building. When the ground shakes and the building tips forward, the computer tells the weight to move in the opposite direction. This stops the building from swaying too far and snapping like a twig.

Another smart system uses electricity and a milky fluid. The fluid forms a layer between the building and its foundation. When sensors pick up the first vibrations, the building's computer turns off electricity in the fluid. This thins the fluid and cushions the building. As shaking goes on, the computer continues to adjust the electricity. The shock waves go back into the ground before they can damage the building.

San Francisco's historic U.S. Court of Appeals building was badly damaged in the 1989 Loma Prieta earthquake. Now it may be one of the most quake-proof buildings anywhere.

The building was raised from its foundation with hydraulic jacks. Special sliding plates were put in place. Then the building was set down again.

The sliding plates are between the building and any ground motion. Now the courthouse should be able to ride out future earthquakes on its new Friction Pendulum System (F.P.S.).

The 837-foot Transamerica Building in San Francisco was built to take quakes. Its triangular framework is supported by steel columns inside concrete.

The wide San Francisco streets should help prevent the spread of fire during an earthquake. They allow space for tall buildings to sway without hitting each other.

Greg Guler feels pretty safe in Disney Studios, where he works. He knows the building is on rollers.

The Salk Institute in San Diego is another place built to take quakes. The buildings have layers of rubber and steel between their walls and foundation. These soften any quake vibrations.

## Try This!

1. Use a board or book as a base. Pile on a high stack of building blocks.
2. Hold and carefully move the base to start an earthquake. Experiment with different moves: side-to-side, jiggling, and gentle rolling or swaying.
3. Watch your tower of blocks. How does it move?

That's how buildings move in an earthquake. When they fall, people get hurt or killed. That's why civil engineers—those who build highways and buildings—want to build things that can ride out a quake.

## Riding Out an Earthquake

Huge rubber and steel pads or giant steel springs under some buildings help soak up a quake's energy. Their bottom floors shift with the ground so the upper floors stay in place.

During an earthquake, a skyscraper can topple if the timing of the building's motion is out of rhythm with the motion of the ground. Strong shaking can begin to move the lower floors, while the upper stories lag behind. If the ground shifts again while the upper stories are still "catching up," the building could snap back and collapse. A building may bend and snap between 15 and 100 times during a typical quake.

# Try This!

1. Stand a Slinky on end on a piece of sandpaper.
2. Grab the edge of the sandpaper. Quickly pull the paper about 6 inches.
3. Watch the Slinky. You will see the bottom of the Slinky pull to the side. The top of the Slinky briefly lags behind and then springs back into place.

That's why buildings with their frames strongly held together are safer in earthquake zones.

# Chapter 10

# Earthquake Survival: What Can You Do?

## Cutting Earthquake Losses

Most earthquake damage and death are caused by falling objects. Chimneys, roofs, walls, bricks, light fixtures, and pictures. Toppling furniture. Flying glass from broken windows. The good news is that earthquake losses can be cut. Three things will make the biggest differences.

- following building codes
- building in safe zones
- community programs that strengthen disaster readiness

Inspecting damage to a garden mall following Loma Prieta quake in 1989

Earthquake damage to kitchen in Coalinga, California

# Staying Safe

Are you concerned about being caught in an earthquake? People get hurt when they panic and don't know what to do. You can be safer. The U.S.G.S. gives these tips.

## Before

1. Take a home-hazard hunt. Go from room to room. Imagine what would happen if the house started shaking. Are there tall bookcases? What things may fall? Which things are heavy enough to hurt people?
2. Make your home safer.
   - Remove heavy objects from shelves that are higher than the height of the shortest family member.
   - Take the fishbowl off the windowsill.
   - Make sure bookshelves, mirrors, and other wall items are fastened tightly to the wall.
   - Put latches on cabinets so they will stay closed during the quake.
   - Make sure there are flexible connectors where gas lines meet so gas lines can't break.
   - Hire someone to bolt refrigerators or hot water heaters in place so they can't fall.
   - Hire someone to bolt the house to the foundation.
   - Make sure your bed is not too close to windows that may break.
   - Outside, remove dead or diseased tree limbs that could fall.
3. Decide where you will go for protection when your house starts to shake. Identify safe spots in each room. Make sure each family member knows where

these areas are. You could be in one part of the house while other family members are in another. And during a violent quake, you won't have time or steady legs to reach them.

4. Hold a family earthquake drill. Call out "EARTHQUAKE" from any place in your home. Each family member should respond by moving to the nearest safe place. Do this often. Test each other.

5. Put together a disaster kit. Include
   - a first-aid kit
   - a battery-operated radio and extra batteries
   - a flashlight
   - a fire extinguisher
   - some simple tools like a crescent wrench (to turn off the gas)
   - water-purification supplies
   - a Coleman stove
   - heavy gloves
   - blankets
   - a battery-operated smoke detector
   - matches
   - stored food and water (Remember to change the food and water every six months.)

6. Learn how to do emergency first aid.

7. Discuss what to expect after a damaging earthquake.

## During

1. Take action at the first sign of shaking.

2. Stay inside. Go to safe places.
   - Under a sturdy table, desk, or kitchen counter. If it moves, move with it!
   - In a wood-framed doorway. The structure above you

will help protect you. But remember, doors may slam shut during an earthquake.
- Against an inside corner or wall. Cover your head with your arms or a pillow.
3. Move away from danger zones.
   - Windows that may shatter.
   - Stove, fireplace, and areas where bricks from the chimney may fall.
   - Bookcases and tall things that may topple.
4. Turn away from windows. Kneel alongside a wall. Bend your head close to your knees. Cover the sides of your head with your elbows. Clasp your hands firmly behind your neck.
5. Do not run outside. Windows and signs can fly off buildings. Buildings, trees, or power lines might fall on you.
6. If you *are* outside, move to an open space away from buildings or power lines. Lie down or crouch to the ground. Keep looking around so you can move if necessary.

## After

1. Don't stay in or near a building that may suffer aftershocks.
2. Stay close enough to touch and comfort each other.
3. Be ready to turn off the gas, water, and power in your house. And learn how to check for gas and water leaks.
4. Talk about how brave and how afraid you were.

# GLOSSARY

| | |
|---|---|
| **Aftershock** | a smaller quake that follows the first quake. |
| **Civil engineers** | those who design buildings and highways. |
| **Crust** | the outer layer of the earth's surface. |
| **Earthquake** | shaking of the earth caused by a sudden movement of rock beneath its surface. |
| **Earthquake zones** | areas where earthquakes are most likely to occur. |
| **Epicenter** | point on the earth's surface directly above the focus of an earthquake. |
| **Fault** | a crack in the earth's crust. |
| **Focus** | the point inside the earth where earthquake vibrations begin; also called the hypocenter. |
| **Love wave** | (L wave) a major type of surface wave. It travels near the surface and causes most of the damage. |
| **Magnitude** | a measure of the strength of an earthquake or energy released by it; shown on a seismograph. |
| **Mantle** | the layer of molten rock under the earth's crust; the zone inside the earth between the solid outer crust and the inner core. |
| **Mercalli Intensity Scale** | twelve-point scale that measures how much damage an earthquake does to land, people, and structures. |
| **Moment-Magnitude Scale** | a scale that measures the total energy released by a quake. |
| **Plate tectonics** | the science concerned with the movement of the earth's crust. |

| | |
|---|---|
| **Plate** | one of the huge sections that make up the earth's crust. |
| **Primary wave** | (P wave) first shock wave to arrive after there is an earthquake; push-pull wave. |
| **Rayleigh wave** | (R wave) a type of surface energy wave. It travels near the earth's surface and causes most of the damage in an earthquake. |
| **Richter Scale** | a number scale from 1 to 9 that measures the amount of shaking energy released during an earthquake. |
| **Ring of Fire** | a large zone of volcanic and seismic activity that roughly follows the borders of the Pacific Ocean; the edges of the earth's crustal plates that almost encircle the Pacific Ocean. |
| **Seismogram** | a written record of an earthquake. |
| **Seismograph** | a device that measures and records vibrations from an earthquake. |
| **Seismologist** | scientist who studies earthquakes. |
| **Shear waves** | (S waves) the secondary waves of an earthquake. They move more slowly than primary waves and shove rocks and materials from side to side. |
| **Tremors** | shaking motions. |
| **Tsunami** | huge sea wave caused by an earthquake on the ocean floor. |

# Index